Dinosaurs
Oviraptor

by Julie Murray

Dash!
LEVELED READERS
An Imprint of Abdo Zoom • abdobooks.com

Level 1 – Beginning
Short and simple sentences with familiar words or patterns for children who are beginning to understand how letters and sounds go together.

Level 2 – Emerging
Longer words and sentences with more complex language patterns for readers who are practicing common words and letter sounds.

Level 3 – Transitional
More developed language and vocabulary for readers who are becoming more independent.

THIS BOOK CONTAINS RECYCLED MATERIALS

abdobooks.com

Published by Abdo Zoom, a division of ABDO, PO Box 398166, Minneapolis, Minnesota 55439. Copyright © 2020 by Abdo Consulting Group, Inc. International copyrights reserved in all countries. No part of this book may be reproduced in any form without written permission from the publisher. Dash!™ is a trademark and logo of Abdo Zoom.

Printed in the United States of America, North Mankato, Minnesota.
052019
092019

Photo Credits: Alamy, Getty Images, iStock, Science Source, Shutterstock, Backyard Terrors Dinosaur Park-Bluff City TN
Production Contributors: Kenny Abdo, Jennie Forsberg, Grace Hansen, John Hansen
Design Contributors: Dorothy Toth, Neil Klinepier

Library of Congress Control Number: 2018963182

Publisher's Cataloging in Publication Data
Names: Murray, Julie, author.
Title: Oviraptor / by Julie Murray.
Description: Minneapolis, Minnesota : Abdo Zoom, 2020 | Series: Dinosaurs | Includes online resources and index.
Identifiers: ISBN 9781532127182 (lib. bdg.) | ISBN 9781532128165 (ebook) | ISBN 9781532128653 (Read-to-me ebook)
Subjects: LCSH: Oviraptor--Juvenile literature. | Dinosaurs--Juvenile literature. | Dinosaurs--Behavior--Juvenile literature.
Classification: DDC 567.912--dc23

Table of Contents

Oviraptor 4

More Facts 22

Glossary 23

Index 24

Online Resources 24

Oviraptor

Oviraptor was a **theropod** dinosaur. It lived 80 million years ago.

It stood 3 feet (0.9 m) tall. It was 6 feet (1.8 m) long. It weighed 60 pounds (27.2 kg).

It had feathers, but it did not fly. Its feathers were bright colors.

It ran on its hind legs. It moved fast. It could run 40 mph (64.4 kph)!

It had a parrot-like head with a **crest** on top. It had a short beak.

Its arms were short. It had long fingers with sharp claws.

It had a long tail. There was a fan of feathers at the end.

It was likely an **omnivore**.

Its **fossils** were first discovered in 1924 in **Mongolia**.

More Facts

- The **crest** on its head could make noises. It warned of danger to others.

- Its name means "egg robber." This is because its **fossils** were first found near eggs. Scientists later learned that these were likely its own eggs.

- The oviraptor laid its eggs in the sand. It sat on them to keep them warm and protect them.

Glossary

crest – a tuft of feathers or bone on an animal's head.

fossil – the remains or trace of a living animal or plant from a long time ago. Fossils are found embedded in earth or rock.

Mongolia – a landlocked country in East Asia. The Gobi Desert, where many incredible fossils have been found, covers southern Mongolia.

omnivore – an animal that lives on a diet of both plants and animals.

theropod – a type of dinosaur characterized by hollow bones and three-toed limbs.

Index

arms 14

beak 13

claws 14

coloring 8

feathers 8, 13, 17

fingers 14

food 19

fossils 21

legs 11

Mongolia 20

size 6

speed 11

tail 17

weight 6

Online Resources

Booklinks
NONFICTION NETWORK
FREE! ONLINE NONFICTION RESOURCES

To learn more about the Oviraptor, please visit **abdobooklinks.com** or scan this QR code. These links are routinely monitored and updated to provide the most current information available.